8/10

DOROTHEA LANGE

HOMER PAGE: DOROTHEA LANGE, 1956.

DOROTHEA LANGE

with an introductory essay by George P. Elliott

THE MUSEUM OF MODERN ART, NEW YORK

in collaboration with the Los Angeles County Museum of Art, the Oakland Museum and the Worcester Art Museum

Distributed by Doubleday & Company, Inc., Garden City, New York

©1966, THE MUSEUM OF MODERN ART, NEW YORK
11 WEST 53 STREET, NEW YORK, N.Y. 10019
LIBRARY OF CONGRESS CATALOGUE
CARD NUMBER: 66-17304
DESIGNED BY JOSEPH BOURKE DEL VALLE
PRINTED IN THE U.S.A.
BY PHOTOGRAVURE AND COLOR, NEW JERSEY

Acknowledgments

The selection of the pictures for this book, and for the exhibition that it accompanies, was in an unusual degree a collaborative effort between the artist and the exhibition director. Basic decisions concerning the content and organization of the exhibition and book were largely agreed on by mid-September of 1965, after discussions extending for well over a year. A few issues were left unresolved at the time of the artist's death on October 11th, and in these cases I have depended on my own understanding of Miss Lange's intention, and on my judgment of her success.

Many people have assisted in the preparation of the exhibition and book, and most must go unnamed. However, I would like to pay special thanks for the outstanding contributions of the following:

To Paul Taylor, for his assistance with editing and research, for his objective memory of the past, and for the sensitivity of his value judgments;

To Daniel and John Dixon, for their frank and selfless contribution to the editing process;

To Richard Conrat, who worked closely with Miss Lange during the two years before her death in organizing her files and making work prints of preliminary editing, and whose assistance in supervising final exhibition prints and in supplying dates and titles has been invaluable;

To Irwin Welcher, who on the basis of the photographer's work prints and notations produced the exhibition prints. This demanding task was begun during the photographer's lifetime, and under her supervision; her judgment of these prints was that they were a full realization of her intention;

To Edgar Breitenbach and The Library of Congress, for loan of negatives from the Farm Security Administration Collection, and for research assistance;

To May E. Fawcett and the National Archives, for loan of negatives from the Bureau of Agricultural Economics and the War Relocation Authority collections;

To Ansel Adams, Shirley Burden, Wayne Miller, and Edward Steichen, whose counsel was deeply valued by Miss Lange and by me;

To Florence Bates Hayward, Therese Heyman, and Nancy Newhall, for valuable research assistance;

To Grace Mayer, Josephine Bradley, and Elita Taylor, for preparation of the bibliography and the chronology;

To Kathleen Haven, for installation of the exhibition; to Joseph Bourke Del Valle, for designing the book.

On behalf of Miss Lange's family, I would also like to thank her many friends and colleagues whose encouragement and devotion helped her meet the heavy demands of this last work.

John Szarkowski
DIRECTOR, DEPARTMENT OF PHOTOGRAPHY

CONTENTS

On Dorothea Lange

The contemplation of things as they are
Without error or confusion
Without substitution or imposture
Is in itself a nobler thing
Than a whole harvest of invention.

FRANCIS BACON

(Dorothea Lange tacked this quotation onto her darkroom door in 1923, where it remained until her death in 1965.)

In every art glancing is an enemy of vision, but in none so much as in photography. Mass journalism has trained us to glance, and the big-money photographers have made themselves masters of the craft of the quick impression: visual elements so whimsically juxtaposed that the effect is to jolt or tickle the viewer, a portrait that makes a famous face look like a dry mud flat but does not penetrate to the person inside this mask which was imposed upon him by the photographer's cleverness.

For a photographer like Dorothea Lange, the problem of the viewer's glancing is especially grave. She avoids technical tricks. She seldom arranges her subjects, and when she does, she does it openly: she has the people look at the camera so that the viewer realizes they are "having their picture taken." The subjects to which she is drawn are unspectacular and ordinary. True, a few of the images in this collection make a bold first impression of the fashionable sort, the hawk-nosed face on page 89, for example, but only if she thought them good second-lookers would she include them in the exhibition representing her life's work.

"That's a second-looker," she would say as she flipped through a pile, and she'd lay the print on the table for a minute or two. You had glanced at it before; but this time you saw it.

But suppose, as is likely, you are leafing through a photography magazine or annual, and come on the photograph of six Texans (page 32). Why should you bother to look twice at some farmers in work clothes lined up in front of a shack gazing at a camera thirty years ago, when not far away you have glancing privileges at a V of wild geese against moonlit clouds or at a dead child at the corner of whose mouth flies are settling? To be sure, if you do look at the farmers twice, you will be likely to look at them more than twice, to go back to them occasionally over the years. You will get to know them, and also something of the world which they helped make but which is no longer theirs. It is the photographer's faith that anything really seen is worth seeing, and to this faith Dorothea Lange adds her own, that anyone really known is worth knowing. But this benefit of seeing, this pleasure and knowledge, can come only if you pause a while, extricate yourself from the madding mob of quick impressions ceaselessly battering us all our lives, and look thoughtfully at a quiet image. Here are six unexceptional men who are kept from the work of their lives, partly by the drought, partly by technology and capitalism, but also by a Success game which makes them not just unfortunates but failures; yet they had no more than the vaguest understanding of the rules of that game which is wrecking them and which in any case they had not been playing. Only by meditation can you see what the photographer is showing.

There are ways to get a viewer to second-look at photographs which do not make a socko first impression, and the photographer can do something about some of these ways. However, the essential pre-condition is beyond his control: the viewer must be willing to pause, to look again, to meditate. Granted this, he must also be told which of the media's myriads to look at twice; he must rely on the authority of editors, museum directors, and other photographers to do most of the selecting for him. About this too, a given photographer can do little. He can play politics, it is true, but not all the wire-pulling and slipper-licking in Babylon will, finally, do a fraction as much to get a picture known and seen as its own power. "Migrant Mother" (page 25) is famous because key people, editors and so on, themselves finding it inexhaustibly rich, have urged the rest of the world to look at it. This picture, like a few others of hers, like a few others of a few other photographers, leads a life of its own. That is, it is widely accepted as a work of art with its own message rather than its maker's; far more people know the picture than know who made it. There is a sense in which a photographer's apotheosis is to become as anonymous as his camera. For an artist like Dorothea Lange who does not primarily aim to make photographs that are ends in themselves, the making of a great, perfect, anonymous image is a trick of grace, about which she can do little beyond making herself available for the gift of that grace. For what she most wants is to see this subject here and now in such a way as to say something about the world.

Granted her impulse to say as well as to see, and granted especially her urgent desire to get her pictures looked at with attention, both for their message and for her own natural pride as an artist, what extension of photographic method, what honest stratagem, was available for her employment?

Context.
Context: a weaving together.

She began to photograph people in the context of their lives.

Until 1932, she had worked as a portrait photographer, picturing people out of context or in the pseudo-context of a studio. A few of these portraits were excellent photographs, but they were very few. From time to time she had tried landscapes, subjects from nature. In that sort of photography, of which her friends Edward Weston and Ansel Adams are masters, exact time and place matter enormously to the working photographer—this spot at this moment—but they matter very little to the viewer. It is a pure art: not this particular tree so much as a perfect image of a tree. But that was not her way.

For she came to realize how deeply her commitment was to people—not just to beautiful or famous people, not just to people who paid her to portray them, but to imperfect people whose actuality was most likely to be realized in the physical and social circumstances in which they were spending their lives. If a picture should turn out to be perfectly beautiful, so much the better. What had come to matter to her most was that a photograph, perfect or not, should say: "Here is what these people are like now." And when she showed objects without people, they were the things by which people had their being, as in her photograph of three churches on the Great Plains (page 52).

By 1932, having mastered her craft so that her camera was an extension of her eye, she went out of her studio onto the risky, uncontrollable streets and looked at the dispossessed, those in whom the life of society was then most visible. "White Angel Breadline, San Francisco, 1933" (page 20) was her first photograph to become widely known and her first important one to provide the viewer with something of the context of the lives of the people in it. What has made the picture celebrated is in large part the image of the unshaven, hunched-up little man in the foreground, leaning on a railing with a tin can between his arms, his hands clenched, the line of his mouth bitter, his back turned to those others waiting for a handout. This image does not derive its power from formal elegance so much as from its being inextricably entangled with the comment it is making. It is art for life's sake.

She was not long in discovering that the fearfulness with which she went out among those strangers was ungrounded. She was not of those she moved among, it is true. She did not see as they saw: a good photographer must have a cold, compositional eye. She did not go looking for the pretty things they would consider it proper for a photographer to look at. But one may conjecture that for the most part they felt that she was with them if not of them (she was often asked if she was part of the government), that her heart was warm, that her sympathies were for them. She asked them only questions she herself would, and did, answer ("How much do you make a year?"), and she paid attention to their answers. What they said became part of the context of what she saw. Here is one of many comments she did not forget: "If I had a camera, I wouldn't waste my film takin' pictures of a man diggin' manure." Still and all, if she wanted to waste her film taking a picture of him, he wouldn't stop her, that was her business.

The photographs she was taking in this new way were so obviously excellent that the photographer Willard Van Dyke, seeing them, wrote about them and exhibited them in his studio in Oakland. There, Paul Taylor, an economics professor at the University of California, was struck by them as documents of the life of the time. In 1935 he got her to work with him in preparing a report on migrant labor in California. Theirs was the first important teaming of social analyst and photographer: their presentation of the problem to the state was so effective as to help produce a direct practical result: the building of camps for the migrants. Moreover, in part because of the Lange-Taylor accomplishment, the federal government included a photographic unit in the agency which began under another name but which is best known as the Farm Security Administration.

In her nearly four years with the FSA, Dorothea Lange did much of her best and most of her best-known work. It was as though she had found a context for herself to work in: with Paul Taylor and with the other FSA photographers (especially Russell Lee and Walker Evans), she was picturing some of the disgracefully invisible people of our society, making them visible to all with humane eyes to see.

But even if the subjects are pictured in the context of their lives, and even if the artist has a working context of her own, what about the photographs themselves? How can they best be shown? For in a real sense the way photographs are grouped and named is a context within which each photograph may acquire a new meaning and which may generate a total meaning of its own.

There is the severe, classical method used by "pure" photographers: each image is presented quite independently of the others on the wall or in the book. This is accomplished by having a uniform presentation of the prints and by identifying them only in a sort of sign language—

"Composition VIII" or "Sunset, Sierra Nevadas" or a handful of those occult symbols that mean much to the technician in every photographer but nothing to the rest of the world. Using this method, the artist does not juxtapose photographs in such a way as to make them comment on one another directly, nor does he organize them in thematic sequences; or if there are such arrangements, they are made so unobtrusively as not to rise far in the viewer's consciousness. Among documentary photographers this method is now unusual. Walker Evans's *American Photographs* (1938) is extraordinary for the severity of its presentation. For a photographer with an urgent need to speak through the photographs, the shortcoming of this method is that the viewer, left on his own, may not hear what the pictures are saying; he may not put the parts together or may put them together in a way alien to the one the photographer intended.

At the other extreme of presentation, there is the method of using photographs to illustrate a text, heighten a story, or demonstrate a thesis. Here, juxtaposition, sequence, and variation in size and format are essential, and the burden of coherence is carried by the verbal commentary. Moreover, the photographer, already subordinate in this mode of presentation, may allow editors to select, print, crop, determine the size and sequence of the photographs, and place them on the page. Even if he does this himself, he does it for the same end which the editors had in mind, and for this external end their judgment may very well be better than his; what is needed for the practical purposes of magazine picture story, illustrated history, advertisement, or propaganda article is calculation not creation, craft not art. For a photographer who is also a serious artist,

the danger of this method of organizing pictures is that the viewer is liable to see in them only what he is told to see.

Dorothea Lange went to neither of these extremes. She had the impulses of the severe artist and of the urgent explainer, and the search for a way to satisfy both impulses was a considerable part of her unceasing restlessness as a photographer, though no method she worked out satisfied her fully. In the thirties, this search was especially urgent; she hoped to ameliorate the social turmoil and injustice by presenting forcefully to the world what she saw. How was she to accomplish this practical end without violating her artist's conscience? How much should she crop the prints? In what order should they appear? What words should accompany them?

Just how important context of this sort can be in governing a photograph's effect may be illustrated by two versions of "Plantation Overseer and His Field Hands" (next page, left and page 48). Complete with the subtitle "Mississippi Delta, 1936," the photograph portrays a ruler among his ruled in a social pattern which both the middle-aged white man and the young colored men obviously know and are existing in without evident strain. The Coca-Cola ad is for all of them; the machine is his and his foot is on it. What they can not realize but what the picture shows, especially clearly to us thirty years later, is that that ad and that car will destroy the whole system of power which seems to the six men in the nature of things. The photograph does not make the usual liberal complaint about this system of power, "How awful this is"; it says something far more subtle and enduring, "This is, and because of the way it is, it will cease to be." In a real sense, the picture with its caption makes its own context.

But, changed and in another context, as number seven (above right) of *Land of the Free* (1938), it says something far less interesting. The four Negroes to the left have been cropped out and the Negro's head under the Coca-Cola ad has been blacked out so that it is featureless. Everything centers upon the white man in front of a country store with his foot up on the bumper of his car; he looks like a plain farmer now. The commentary for the book (thirty-three of the eighty-eight photographs are Dorothea Lange's) is a poem by Archibald MacLeish. Some of the opposite-page text which transforms this Southern man of power into an American man of freedom is as follows:

> We told ourselves we were free
>   because we were free.
> We were free because we were that kind.
> We were Americans.
>
> All you needed for freedom was being American.
> All you needed for freedom was grit in your craw
>
> And the gall to get out on a limb
>   and crow before sunup.
> Those that hadn't it hadn't it.

Opposite the whole photograph, these words would have been ironic. Opposite the partial photograph, the words are straight, so that the simpler, partial picture among the other photographs in that book has come to have a meaning profoundly opposed (and inferior) to that of the whole, complex picture.

In *An American Exodus* (1940), Dorothea Lange and Paul Taylor in collaboration created a context of words and pictures which came closest to saying what they then had to say. The 115 photographs, all but nine of which are hers, are grouped thematically: Old South, Plantation Under the Machine, Midcontinent, and so on. They often speak in juxtaposition and sequence. The format is uniform. All are the width of the page and face you as you hold the book in the usual reading position; none contrast shockingly and there are no double-page spreads; they differ only in length, from a quarter page to a full page. Some of them are not good second-lookers but are there to illustrate the text. The words consist of quotations from the people themselves or from newspapers and magazines, of some commentary in severely objective analytic prose, and of neutral identifications ("Small Independent Gas Station During Cotton Strike, Kern City, November, 1938") (page 37). This is the fastidious way which the photographer and analyst found between art's non-interference and persuasion's control.

But she did not use this method again. She became less concerned with making a context of persuasion for her photographs and more with making them themselves. After all, most of the act of photographic creation consists in opening a shutter at the right place at the right instant, and most of the remainder of this creation is printing (and perhaps cropping). Such contexts as she made of and for her pictures were aids to contemplation—for example, a portfolio of thirty pictures entitled "The American Country Woman." When she learned that she was fatally ill, that she had done almost all the work permitted her (she regretted not being able to help document the sixties as she had done the thirties), she devoted her last year to printing and arranging the photographs which were her life's work.

Each one not only had to say something but had to say it well and irrespective of whether it was documentary. The old woman "Rebecca Dixon" (page 68), for example, need not be identified by nationality, year, or station in life: she is *there* in the world, unmistakably herself. Of the many images of women which Dorothea Lange caught on film, this one was to survive the artist's judging eye, because that old woman is *there* on paper too. The image has a life congruous to the woman's own living strength. A chance of light became her: the artist saw this and translated chemically what she saw into an image: we may see it too.

When one is thinking of photographs in this way, it is hard to put them into contexts of meanings that direct the viewer away from the image before him towards the life which the image represents. In this book, the images and their titles create their own context; what unifies them is their maker. Ultimately a good photographer speaks through his pictures. He says what you see, whatever he may say about what you see. Context dissolves into vision.

When Dorothea Lange looks into a camera, she does not, as many do, find forms abstracted from meaning; or, if she does find them, she has not displayed them. Nor is her primary purpose to arrange recognizable objects into formally pleasing patterns. One must be a bit cautious in making such generalizations. It is true that the pleasure some of the photographs offer is only incidentally formal (see pages 37, 51, 54). It is equally true that many others give much formal gratification (see pages 28, 52, 69, or the great "Migrant Mother," page 25). But not one of all these photographs, except perhaps for the portrait of the Pathan Warrior Tribesman (page 89), would survive abstracting into pure form, as some of Weston's do; and even the picture is far richer as a person seen than as a confluence of dark and gleaming swirls. The Warrior Tribesman at one end, the sign in the small town gas station at the other—such is the range of this artist's vision. It is a vision which will not detach from what it sees. Form and subject both serve it.

Often she looks so hard at the ordinary that it fills with seeing. The work on page 91 recalls van Gogh's painting of a pair of work shoes on flagstones; there is far more vitality in those shoes than in most lords and ladies in portraits, because they have been seen utterly. Similarly, the bare foot in her photograph is seen to the very limit of the power of film to catch and hold the seeing. Smoothed out, touched up, that image would have little interest.

"First Born" (page 74) relies less upon the technical aspects of photography, for it is a referential picture, humanly rich as well as formally satisfying. There is no background. The young man's serious face is not strongly characterized: he is The Young Father. The real focus of attention is on his strong hands at once holding and offering, as it were, a holy thing, the bundle containing his baby. The picture does not need, and indeed suffers from, local context. It serves as handsomely the universal context of Edward Steichen's *The Family of Man* (1955) as it serves this collection of the artist's work; but neither of these collections serves it in return. Just as photography takes an instant out of time, altering life by holding it still, so the artifice of this image takes this young man out of the accidents and shifts of his life and holds him still, blurring him a little, so that our understanding may penetrate, not to his particular self, but to the artist's vision of what he incarnates at this instant.

"Vision" has religious or mystical overtones. Yet no art is less mystical, by its nature, than photography, especially referential photography. Chemical and photomechanical processes are purely secular. The appearances of actual things, which comprise photography's subject matter, are by definition superficial and often illusory or deceptive as well. When to these limitations one adds Dorothea Lange's resolve to photograph only unmanipulated scenes from ordinary life, many of them tied to a here and now, one begins

to appreciate how difficult a task she undertook and how marvelous it is that the word vision can be used of her work at all, or of her as we know her through her work.

It hardly applies to the pictures which are entirely documentary. The photograph on page 49 is an admirable image of the front of a Southern country store in the late thirties. In a person who was there, it can generate a powerful nostalgia. For one who did not know that way of life, it affords an obviously faithful glimpse which has more to do with artifacts than with relationships. The "Plantation Overseer and His Field Hands" (page 48) is of a similar subject, one white man and five Negroes in front of a store in the South during the Depression, but it documents less and penetrates further. It shows fewer things but reveals their relationships better. Both of these photographs—indeed, all in this book—invite one primary response which is true of any vision however secular or religious: attention. "Here is something in the world worthy of your attention," each photograph says, pointing at its subject. And to this one may add, pointing at the picture itself, "Whatever else you feel, pain, outrage, joy, amusement, bewilderment, as you attend to this picture, you will also have the pleasure of paying attention well. You will, if you want to, see clearly, just for the sake of seeing."

Occasionally her vision is of artifacts and reveals something of a culture—"Highway 40" (page 83), for example, the irony of which speaks to any American, a truckload of new cars racing on a highway above smoldering junked cars in an unnatural landscape. Usually her vision is of people—faces, feet, hands, bodies—so caught that one needs to know their social context in order fully to comprehend the significance of the expressions or gestures; "The Defendant" (page 78), for example, and "Ditched, Stalled and Stranded" (page 26) need descriptive titles at least to be all there. Nearly always her vision is of a complexity, doubleness, ambiguity, which forbids an easy, rehearsed response—in the photograph on page 43, the expression on the face of the Negro woman field-worker, humorous and shrewd rather than hopeless and pitiable, or the handsome pattern made by the furrows which have emptied the pathetic shanty in "Tractored Out" (page 24). "Egyptian Village, 1963" (page 102) is a kind of test case. How can an American interpret the complex expression on this Egyptian's face without knowing the meaning of those other people's hands, one laid on and one descending towards his head? But it is possible that the photographer herself did not know what this meant. If you had been there—and if you had been able to glance with her attention—this may have been as much as you would have seen at that instant. In any case, for an American to see this picture is for him to see a man in some sort of distress and to realize just how profoundly we rely upon cultural cues in order to understand one another. Is he mad? moronic? holy? clowning? suffering physical pain? mugging as the photographer paid him to? begging? threatening? A considerable part of the fascination of this image is that it raises such perplexities without decreasing our pleasure in the image itself. Whatever is going on there in the world, it is worth paying attention to here in the picture.

A paradox: glancing is a foe of art, yet a person walking around in the world with a camera in his hand must see in glances. A camera shutter does not glance so much as superglance. Glancing for so short a time, it takes out of our kind of time what it sees.

The photograph, "Migratory Cotton Picker, Eloy, Arizona, 1940" (page 28), for example, of a young man with his hand, palm out, across the lower part of his face: it was the lens, not the photographer's eye, that caught this exact instant. Not even in the view finder could she have seen all that we see here in this print. These are greys, that was in color. Doubtless he was in motion, speaking, gesturing, looking about; she could not have known the exact relationship of his hand to his face as it would seem in a photograph. She could not have known—she a small woman with a reflex camera hanging from her neck, shuffling back and forth near a ranch hand she is also talking to and listening to—she could not possibly have known the contrasting effect of textures, especially the dull palm and the glistening face, as it appears in the print. Quite likely she took a good many shots of him, as she had taken many of other subjects, and afterwards was grateful to find this one on the film.

What she could see, as she there on the ranch was preparing her camera to do its special glancing, was potentials. She knew and felt that it was possible for the light to catch him just right—the sadness we see in the eyes is an effect of shadow. She knew and felt that there was an unconscious gesture he could make from his own being which could reveal to the camera's glance something essential about that being. She kept stepping about in the hope that these possibilities would collect themselves in one unselfconscious revelation while the lens was ready. She made herself accessible to the operations of grace. She had done and was to do this many many times without avail: this time she was lucky, as she was a few dozen other times in her life.

Chance (in the form of her husband's profession) took her to Asia in 1958 and to Egypt in 1963. From these visits she brought back some fine images: the perfection of serenity in the face of "Korean Child" (page 94), the probably ordinary face made mysterious by the veil (page 98), the foot (page 91), the suspicious eyes staring at this alien (page 93), the complex and revealing beauty of the walking man's posture (page 101). What was ordinary to the ordinary people she was looking at was extraordinary to her, and under such circumstances anyone is likely to be able to see in a glance more than he normally sees in a glance at home. She walked about in the world full of interest, compassion, and a sense of the complexity of things. She could look at a print with a ruthless eye. But alone, these were not enough for the making of great images. She needed a sense of the marvelous in what she looked at, and this sense was quickened, late in her life, especially by some extraordinary ordinary people in Egypt.

Not until she knew she had a limited time left to live did she agree to exhibit a comprehensive collection of her photographs either in a museum or in a book. In a true artist the work is the life. There are those who learn what they can do well and then do only that, but she could never be satisfied that she had seen all there was for her to see.

Though her vision is not obviously religious, perhaps these four lines from Blake's *Auguries of Innocence* suggest something of it.

God appears, and God is Light,
To those poor souls who dwell in Night;
But does a Human Form display
To those who dwell in realms of Day.

HOPI INDIAN, NEW MEXICO. c. 1923

MEXICAN-AMERICAN, SAN FRANCISCO. 1928

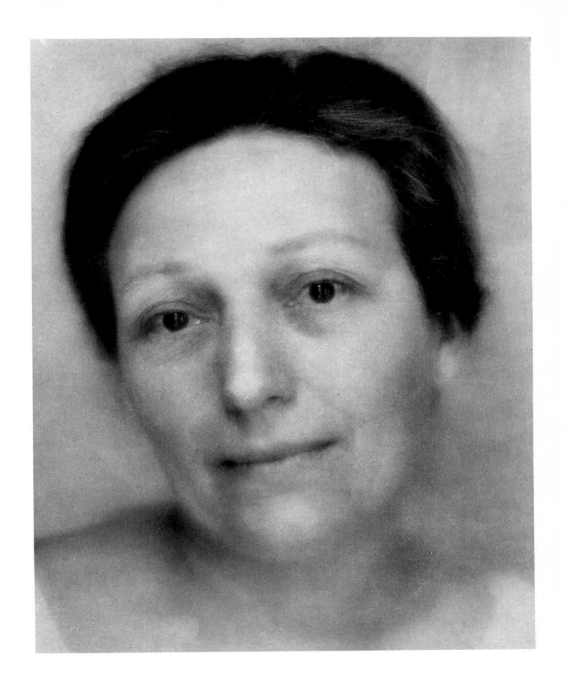

ADELE RAAS, SAN FRANCISCO.   c. 1920

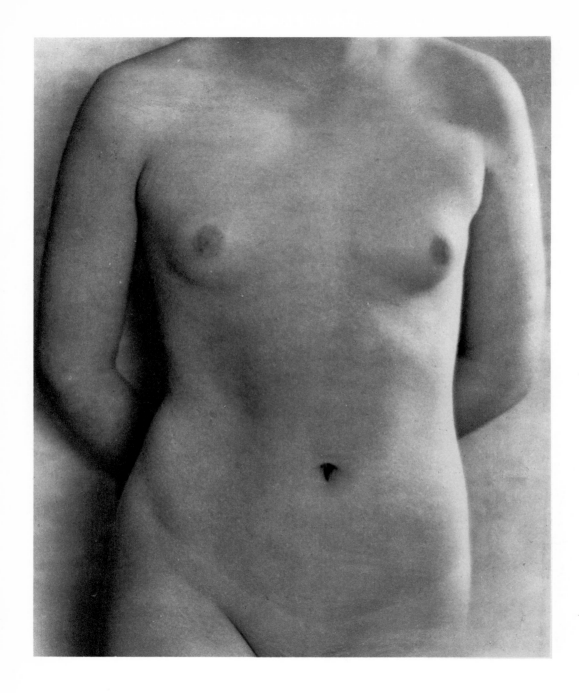

TORSO, SAN FRANCISCO. 1923

JOHN, SAN FRANCISCO. 1931

WHITE ANGEL BREADLINE, SAN FRANCISCO.   1933

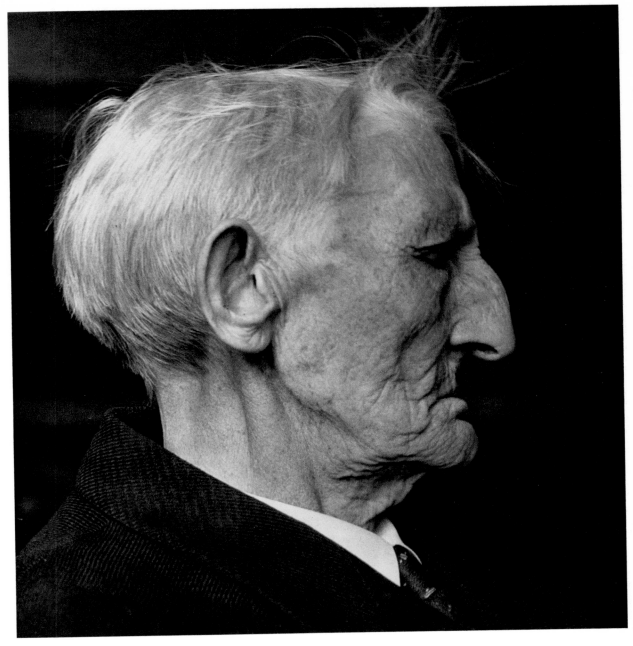

ANDREW FURUSETH, SAN FRANCISCO. 1934

STREET DEMONSTRATION, SAN FRANCISCO. 1933

FUNERAL CORTEGE, END OF AN ERA IN A SMALL VALLEY TOWN, CALIFORNIA. 1938

TRACTORED OUT, CHILDRESS COUNTY, TEXAS. 1938

OPPOSITE: MIGRANT MOTHER, NIPOMO, CALIFORNIA. 1936 (RA)

DITCHED, STALLED AND STRANDED, SAN JOAQUIN VALLEY, CALIFORNIA. 1935 (RA)

DAMAGED CHILD, SHACKTOWN, ELM GROVE, OKLAHOMA. 1936

MIGRATORY COTTON PICKER, ELOY, ARIZONA. 1940 (BAE)

CHILD AND HER MOTHER, WAPATO, YAKIMA VALLEY, WASHINGTON. 1939 (FSA)

YOUNG MIGRATORY COTTON PICKER, CASA GRANDE, ARIZONA. 1940

WOMAN IN MIGRATORY LABOR CAMP, CALIFORNIA. 1938. (FSA)

SIX TENANT FARMERS WITHOUT FARMS, HARDMAN COUNTY, TEXAS. 1938 (FSA)

A HALF-HOUR LATER, HARDMAN COUNTY, TEXAS.   1938

BACK. 1938

BACK. 1935

JOBLESS ON EDGE OF PEAFIELD, IMPERIAL VALLEY, CALIFORNIA. 1937 (FSA)

KERN COUNTY, CALIFORNIA. 1938

OPPOSITE: WOMAN OF THE HIGH PLAINS, TEXAS PANHANDLE.   1938

TEXAS PANHANDLE.   1938

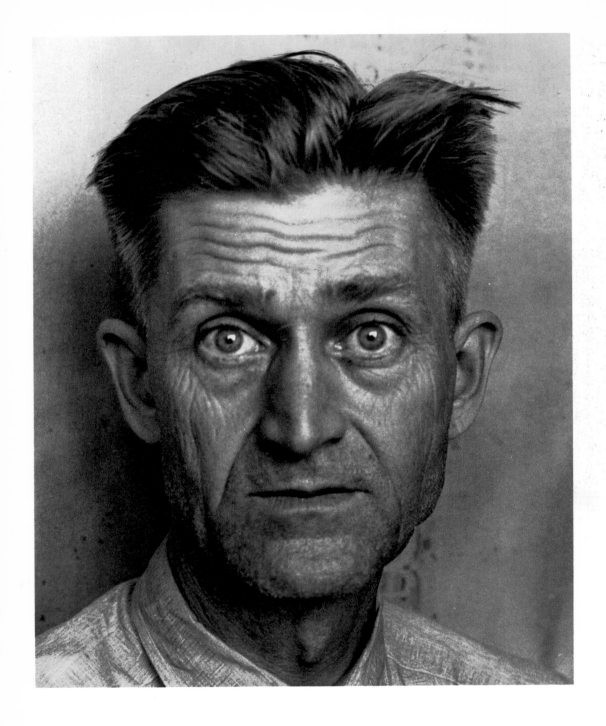

OPPOSITE: J. R. BUTLER, PRESIDENT OF THE SOUTHERN TENANT FARMERS' UNION,
MEMPHIS, TENNESSEE. 1938

GRAYSON, SAN JOAQUIN VALLEY, CALIFORNIA. 1938

SHARECROPPERS, EUTAH, ALABAMA.   1937   (FSA)

OPPOSITE: EX-SLAVE WITH LONG MEMORY, ALABAMA.   1937

HOEING, NEAR YAZOO CITY, MISSISSIPPI. 1937 (FSA)

ONE MAN, ONE MULE, GREENE COUNTY, GEORGIA.   1937   (FSA)

WATER BOY, MISSISSIPPI DELTA.   1938

OPPOSITE: GREENVILLE, MISSISSIPPI.   1938

PLANTATION OVERSEER AND HIS FIELD HANDS, MISSISSIPPI DELTA. 1936 (RA)

CROSSROADS STORE, ALABAMA. 1937

BY THE CHINABERRY TREE, NEAR TIPTON, GEORGIA. 1938

SHERIFF, WAGGONER, OKLAHOMA. 1937 (FSA)

OPPOSITE: ON THE GREAT PLAINS, NEAR WINNER, SOUTH DAKOTA.   1938

THE ROAD WEST, NEW MEXICO.   1938

RICHMOND, CALIFORNIA. 1942

OPPOSITE: ONE NATION INDIVISIBLE, SAN FRANCISCO. 1942 (WRA)

SHIPYARD CONSTRUCTION WORKERS, RICHMOND, CALIFORNIA.   1942

RICHMOND, CALIFORNIA.   1942

ARGUMENT IN TRAILER COURT.   1944

OPPOSITE: OAKLAND, CALIFORNIA.   1942

SHIPYARD WORKER, RICHMOND, CALIFORNIA. 1942

END OF SHIFT, RICHMOND, CALIFORNIA. 1942

TOQUERVILLE, UTAH. 1953

63

TOQUERVILLE, UTAH. 1953

SPRING IN NEW YORK. 1952

SPRING IN BERKELEY. 1951

OPPOSITE: MAN STEPPING FROM CURB. 1956

GUNLOCK, UTAH. 1953

REBECCA DIXON, SAUSALITO. 1954

OAK, BERKELEY. 1957

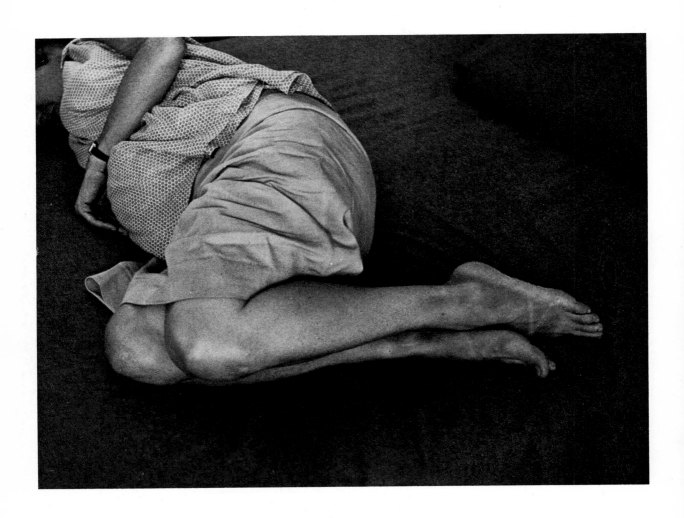

WINTER, CALIFORNIA. 1955

OPPOSITE: BAD TROUBLE OVER THE WEEKEND. 1964

JOHN AND HELEN, BERKELEY. 1955

ANDREW, BERKELEY. 1959

FIRST BORN, BERKELEY. 1952

SECOND BORN, BERKELEY. 1955

"GUILTY, YOUR HONOR," ALAMEDA COUNTY COURTHOUSE, CALIFORNIA.   c. 1955-57

BLACK MARIA, OAKLAND.   c. 1955-57

THE DEFENDANT, ALAMEDA COUNTY COURTHOUSE, CALIFORNIA.   c. 1955-57

THE PUBLIC DEFENDER, ALAMEDA COUNTY COURTHOUSE, CALIFORNIA. c. 1955-57

WALKING WOUNDED, OAKLAND. 1954

TERRIFIED HORSE, NAPA COUNTY, CALIFORNIA. 1956

CAFÉ NEAR PINOLE, CALIFORNIA. 1956

U.S. HIGHWAY #40, CALIFORNIA. 1956

COUNTY CLARE, IRELAND. 1954

COUNTRY ROAD, COUNTY CLARE, IRELAND. 1954

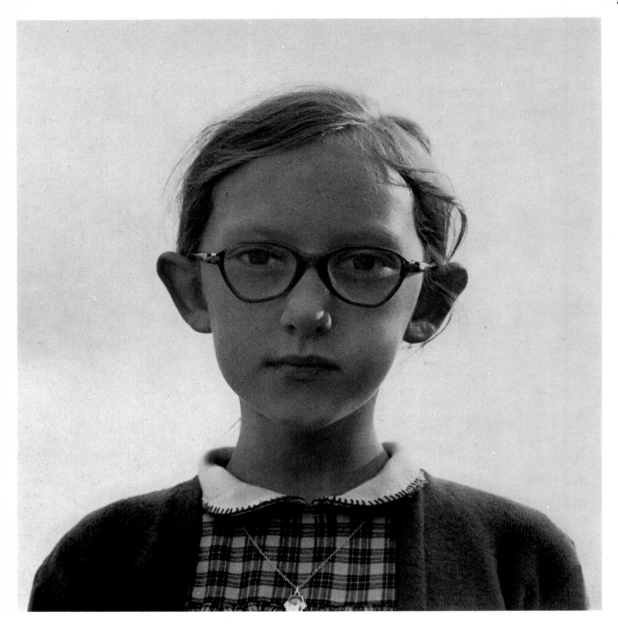

IRISH CHILD, COUNTY CLARE, IRELAND. 1954

STORY TELLER, COUNTY CLARE, IRELAND. 1954

RAINY DAY, COUNTY CLARE, IRELAND. 1954

PATHAN WARRIOR TRIBESMAN, KHYBER PASS.   1958

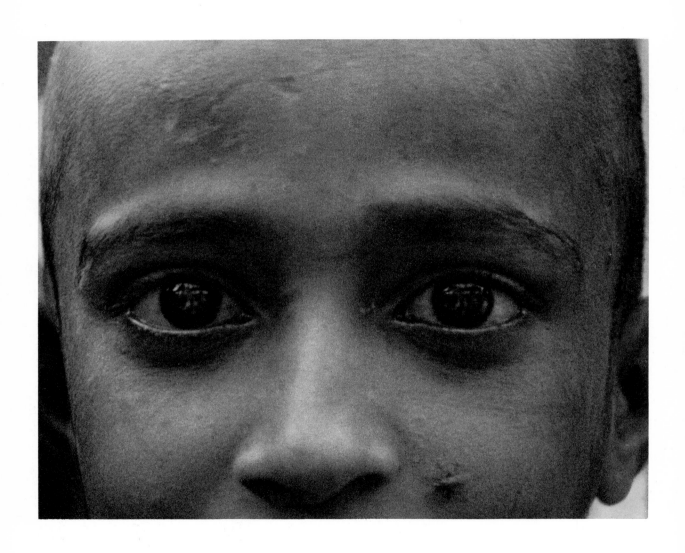

PAKISTANI YOUTH, KARACHI. 1958

opposite: FOOT OF PRIEST, BURMA. 1958

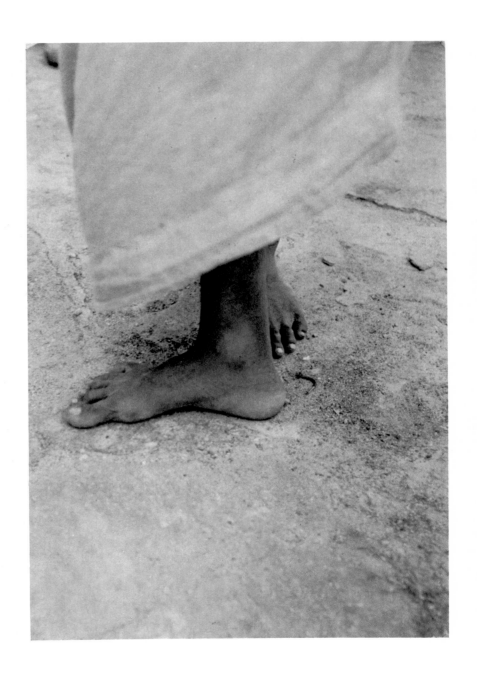

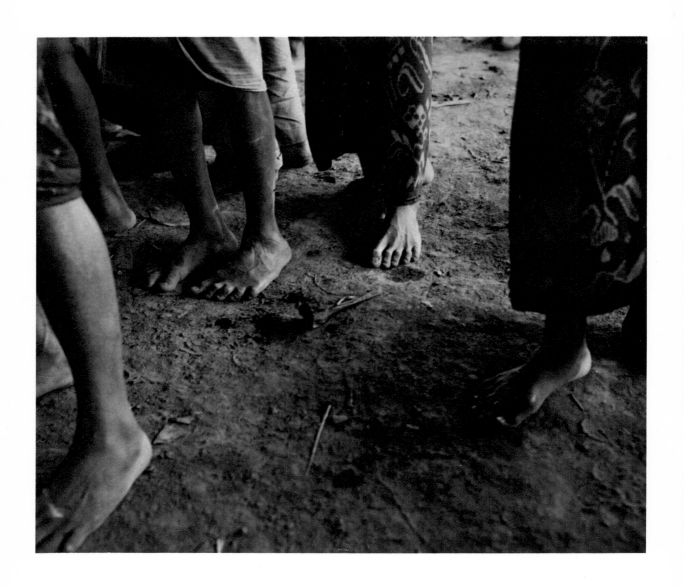

INDONESIA. 1958

HONG KONG. 1958

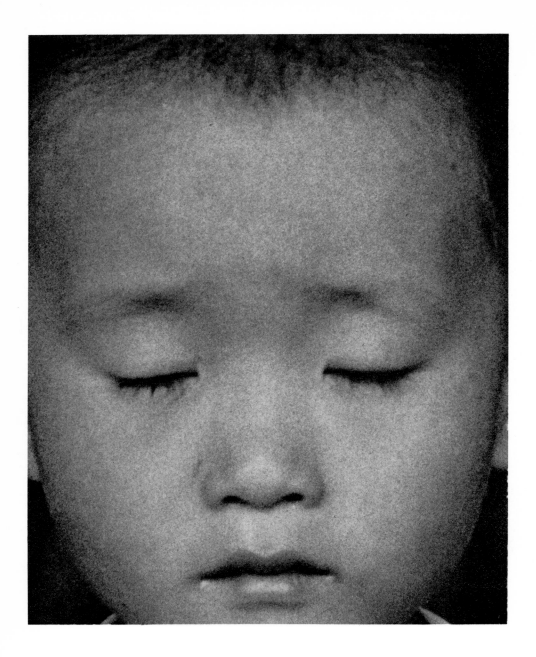

KOREAN CHILD. 1958

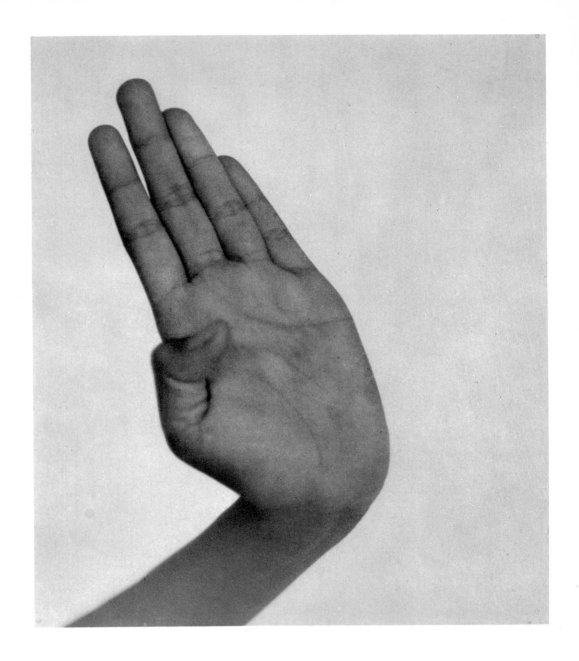

HAND, INDONESIAN DANCER, JAVA. 1958

CAMPESINO, VENEZUELA. 1960

PROCESSION BEARING FOOD TO THE DEAD, UPPER EGYPT. 1963

WOMAN IN PURDAH, UPPER EGYPT. 1963

ARCHITECTURAL DETAIL, UPPER EGYPT. 1963

NILE VILLAGE, EGYPT. 1963

NILE DELTA, EGYPT. 1963

EGYPTIAN VILLAGE. 1963

Notes

The following abbreviations are used after the picture titles to indicate the agency for which the picture was made:
RA: Resettlement Administration (Library of Congress); FSA: Farm Security Administration (Library of Congress); BAE: Bureau of Agricultural Economics (National Archives); WRA: War Relocation Authority (National Archives). Where a quotation is associated with a particular photograph, the text was chosen by Lange as a relevant caption for the picture.

PAGES 15 & 17   These are reproduced from modern prints in which the photographer utilized only a small part of the complete negative. Lange considered cropping to be an important and natural photographic control, and frequently redefined her earlier pictures by reframing.

PAGE 21   Andrew Furuseth was a leading figure of the generation that shaped the American Federation of Labor under Samuel Gompers. He was Secretary of the Sailors Union of the Pacific from near its beginning in the 1880s. Faced with a labor injunction, and jail sentence if convicted of violation, Furuseth responded: "They can't put me in a smaller room than I've always lived in. They can't give me plainer food than I've always eaten. They can't make me any lonelier than I've always been." (Paul S. Taylor, *Sailors Union of the Pacific,* 1923.)

PAGE 22   "This was just before the New Deal during a time when the Communists were very active. A few blocks away, at the waterfront, soup was being distributed daily to the many unemployed." (Dorothea Lange, unpublished notes.)

PAGE 24   "Tractors replace not only mules but people. They cultivate to the very door of the houses of those whom they replace." (P.S.T. & D.L., *An American Exodus,* 1939.)

PAGE 25   "In a squatter camp at the edge of the pea fields. The crop froze this year and the family is destitute. On this morning they had sold the tires from their car to pay for food. She is thirty-two years old." (D.L., unpublished notes.)

PAGE 28   "Resting at cotton wagon before returning to work in the field. He has been picking cotton all day. A good picker earns about two dollars a day working, at this time of the year, about ten hours. This is in an area of rapidly expanding commercial cotton culture." (D.L., unpublished notes.)

PAGE 32   Mechanization stripped the land of families. "All displaced tenant farmers. The oldest thirty-three. All native Americans, none able to vote because of Texas poll tax. All on WPA. They support an average of four persons each on $22.80 a month. '...I can count twenty-three farmers in the west half of this county that have had to leave the farms to give three men more land.' " (P.S.T. & D.L., *An American Exodus.*)

PAGE 36   "That season the winter pea crop froze. He had waited for weeks; then more weeks to wait for the second crop." (D.L., unpublished notes.)

PAGES 38 & 39   "...A lion does not write a book, nor does the weather erect a monument at the place where the pride of a woman was broken for want of a pair of shoes, or where a man worked five years in vain to build a home and gave it up, bankrupt and whipped...or where the wife went insane from sheer monotony and blasted hope." (J. Russell Smith, *North America, 1925.* Quoted in *An American Exodus.*)

PAGE 40 "The Southern Tenant Farmers' Union was organized in Poinsett County, Arkansas, in 1934 in protest over the Government crop-and acreage-restriction programs....J. R. Butler, a country school teacher and farmer sharecropper, became president of the organization." (Stuart Jamieson, *Labor Unionism in American Agriculture, 1945.*)

PAGE 41 "Grayson was a migratory agricultural laborers' shack-town. It was during the season of the pea harvest. Late afternoon about 6 o'clock. Boys were playing baseball in the road that passes this building, which was used as a church. Otherwise, this corpse, lying at the church door, was alone, unattended, and unexplained." (D.L., unpublished notes.)

PAGE 50 Lange recorded the comments of the man in the picture as follows:
The pig - she took up and 'cided she warn't goin no fudder.
I got her dis far.
De value of her would run close to 39 - 40 dollas.
I'd rather take a week to get er thar dan lose her.
I'm 48 years old, and ain't comin forward - it's goin de other way.
That woman live wid me and I live wid her and she's my hesitate.
There's places I just love to see where I've ben before, but I'm gettin old now.

Lots of folks know a lot of scratching of the pen, but they haven't got the wit to back up the pronouncements of it.
Where people's runnin away from work, that's the place for me.
Ah don' like dis yer pushin' and pullin'. (D.L., unpublished notes.)

PAGE 55 "Rafael Weill Elementary School, San Francisco, 1942. Two days before the Army evacuated all persons of Japanese ancestry from the Pacific Coast." (D.L., unpublished notes.)

PAGE 58 "Young war workers, transplanted and in a strange town, angered and miserable." (D.L., unpublished notes.)

PAGE 60 "Wartime shipyard construction brings women into the labor market." (D.L., unpublished notes.)

PAGE 81 "The early winter was a period of catastrophe for the animals of Berryessa Valley. The U.S. Bureau of Reclamation had built a dam at the head of the Valley and had bulldozed the future lake site clear of buildings and vegetation." (D.L., unpublished notes.)

PAGE 82 Rapid development of a previously rural area was occurring. The man at the counter said "Dammit, it's getting so a person can't stand still in one of these here fields without you getting mowed down, raked up, or painted." (D.L., unpublished notes.)

PAGE 87 "Overlooking his house and acres stands one of the magnificent stone ruins from an ancient past. I asked 'How old might this castle be?' 'Madam, we are much too young to know,' he answered." (D.L., unpublished notes.)

Chronology

1895
May 26, born in Hoboken, N. J., of German ancestry.

Attends P. S. 62 on the Lower East Side. Mother works for New York Public Library and in the Juvenile Courts of Jersey City.

c. 1913
Graduates from Wadleigh High School, New York City.

c. 1914-17
Attends the New York Training School for Teachers.

c. 1915
Having decided to become a photographer, visits Arnold Genthe's studio at 562 Fifth Avenue. He encourages her, presents her with first camera and makes critical evaluation of her work over the next year or so.
She works briefly in a portrait studio.

1917-18
Acting on Genthe's advice, she takes a basic photography course given by Clarence H. White at Columbia University.
Rents chicken coop on the Palisades for use as darkroom.

1918
January, hoping to work her way around the world as a photographer, accompanied by her friend Florence Ahlstrom, she sails to New Orleans, then on to El Paso, Los Angeles and San Francisco, where a pickpocket leaves them only $5.
She works as a photo finisher at Marsh Photo Supply House on Market Street and joins camera club on Market Street for darkroom privileges.

1919
Opens a portrait studio in the rear of Irwin Furman's Hill Tollerton Print Room at 540 Sutter Street, which meets with immediate success.

1920
March 21, marries the painter Maynard Dixon.

1925
May 15, Daniel Rhodes Dixon is born.

1928
June 12, John Eaglefeather Dixon is born.

c. 1928
Moves studio from 716 Montgomery Street, where she was for about three years, to 802 Montgomery Street, the crossroads of Chinatown, the Barbary Coast, the wholesale market district and the financial district.

1931-33
Spends a summer near Lake Tahoe with family; spends six months at Ranchos de Taos and Taos, N.M.; travels in Utah, Nevada and Arizona.

1933
Makes the photograph "White Angel Breadline."

1934
Willard Van Dyke exhibits her work in his Oakland studio, 683 Brockhurst Street, and writes an article about her in *Camera Craft*. Paul S. Taylor, an economics professor at the University of California, sees the exhibition and uses one of her photographs in the article "San Francisco and the General Strike" in the September 1934 issue of *Survey Graphic*.
Later by arrangement of Van Dyke a party of photographers including Lange helps Taylor document the Unemployed Exchange Association which was operating a saw-mill. Some of these photographs were used by Taylor in an exhibition at University of California. The prints are now in the Bancroft Library there.
Moves studio to her residence, 2515 Gough Street.

1935
Her increased interest in documentary photography and a lessening demand for portraits lead her, about February 1, to join staff of Paul Taylor

who was now Field Director for the California State Emergency Relief Administration, Division of Rural Rehabilitation. Her photographs support Taylor text recommending camps for migratory agricultural workers. Is listed on table of organization as "typist."

1935-42
In July or August, she transfers to Roy E. Stryker's unit of the Resettlement Administration under Rexford Guy Tugwell. Works full time for RA until 1937, at which time it becomes the Farm Security Administration; from 1937 until 1939 she works part-time; and then occasionally until 1942. (The unit is transferred to the Office of War Information in 1943.)

1935
Meets Pare Lorentz who inspired by her photographs includes California sequence in *The Plow That Broke the Plains* (released 1936). She works with him on film for one day.
October, is divorced from Maynard Dixon.
December 6, marries Paul Taylor.

1936
Makes photograph "Migrant Mother."
Summer, does field work with Paul Taylor, now with Social Security Board.

1938-39
Winter, she and Taylor work on *An American Exodus: A Record of Human Erosion* which is published later in year.

1940
Does special assignments for the U.S. Bureau of Agricultural Economics.
Moves from 2706 Virginia Avenue in San Francisco to 1163 Euclid Avenue in Berkeley.

1941
Is awarded a Guggenheim Fellowship to do a "photographic study of the American social scene." Gives it up after the outbreak of the war.

1940-41
December 31 - January 12, work is first exhibited at The Museum of Modern Art. "Migrant Mother" included in a show of recent acquisitions.

1942
Works for the War Relocation Authority photographing Japanese-Americans being evacuated from the Pacific Coast.

1943-45
Works for the Office of War Information. All her negatives from these years lost in transit.

1945
April 25 - June 26, photographs the United Nations Conference in San Francisco for State Department.
Afterwards, becomes ill and remains in Berkeley relatively inactive until 1950.

1951
Begins to photograph again.
Conducts a seminar at the California School of Fine Arts (now the San Francisco Art Institute).
September 26 - October 6, participates in a Photo-Conference at Aspen, Colorado.

1952-53
November 26 - March 1, 36 photographs included in "Diogenes with a Camera II" at The Museum of Modern Art, New York.

1953
Works with Ansel Adams and her writer son Daniel Dixon in Utah on assignment for *Life* ("Three Mormon Towns," September 6, 1954).

1954
Goes to Ireland with Daniel Dixon on assignment for *Life* ("The Irish Country People," March 21, 1955).

1955
Begins work on several essays in California: "The Public Defender," "On Security" and "On Justice."

January 26 - May 8, 9 photographs included in "The Family of Man" exhibition at The Museum of Modern Art.

1956-57
Photographs the devastation of the Berryessa Valley with Pirkle Jones.
The essay "Death of a Valley" published in *Aperture* in 1960; exhibited at the San Francisco Museum of Art, November 2 - December 4, 1960, and at the Art Institute of Chicago, January 26 - March 3, 1963.

1958-59
June through January, accompanies Taylor in Asia where he is consultant to U. S.—International Cooperation Administration.

1958
Gives several critiques and one seminar at the San Francisco Art Institute where she is also member of informal advisory group until 1962.

1960
Goes to Venezuela and Ecuador with Taylor who is studying agrarian reform and community development for the United Nations.
June 5 - July 8, "La Donna Rurale Americana di Dorothea Lange" is exhibited at the Biblioteca Communale in Milan, Italy.

1961
March, one-man exhibition at the Siembab Gallery in Boston.

1962
January 15 - February 24, her work is included in "USA FSA: Farm Security Administration Photographs of the Depression Era" at the Allen R. Hite Art Institute, University of Louisville.
October 18 - November 25, 85 photographs are included in "The Bitter Years" at The Museum of Modern Art.
December, joins Taylor who is visiting professor at the University of Alexandria, Egypt.

1963
Recurrent illness in Middle and Near East, finally diagnosed as malaria; returns in September.
May 29, is placed on Honor Roll of the American Society of Magazine Photographers.

1964
Works toward retrospective exhibition of her work at The Museum of Modern Art to open January 25, 1966.
Spring, goes to Washington and New York; proposes independent documentary unit to record American urban life.
August, illness diagnosed as cancer of the esophagus.
Completes the portfolio "The American Country Woman."
Works with KQED (San Francisco) on two 30-minute films for the National Educational Television and Radio Center.

1965
October 11, dies of cancer.

A Selected Bibliography

WORKS BY LANGE
(arr. chronologically)

1. LANGE, DOROTHEA. A selection of some of the best photographs of migrant workers, 1935-1936. *In* U.S. Library of Congress. Selective checklist of prints and photographs. Lot no.4699, p.65.
   51 photographs with text. - Photographs made by Lange for the Resettlement Administration.

2. _____ . "Lucretia Penny." Pea-picker's child. *Survey graphic* v.24, no.7:352-353, July 1935.
   Lange photographs.

3. _____ & PAUL SCHUSTER TAYLOR. An American exodus. A record of human erosion. New York, Reynal & Hitchcock, 1939. 158 p.
   Review: *U.S.camera* v.1, no.9:62-63, 71, May 1940.

4. _____ . Documentary photography. *In* San Francisco. Palace of Fine Arts. A pageant of photography. San Francisco, Crocker-Union, [1940]. p.29-30 ill.
   Includes Lange photographs.

5. _____ & ANSEL ADAMS. Fortune's wheel. *Fortune* v.31, no.2:10, February 1945. Pacific coast issue. - In same issue: The golden west, p.116. - After the battle, p.176, 178. - Richmond took a beating, p.262, 264-265, 267-269.

6. _____ & DANIEL DIXON. Photographing the familiar. *Aperture* v.1, no.2:4-15, 1952.
   Includes Lange photographs.

7. _____ . Miss Lange's counsel: photographer advises use of picture themes. *New York Times,* December 7, 1952. Section II, p.23.

8. _____ & ANSEL ADAMS. Three Mormon towns. *Life* v.37, no.10:91-100, September 6, 1954.
   Text by Daniel Dixon.

9. _____ . Irish country people. *Life* v.38, no.12:135-143, March 21, 1955.
   Lange photographs.

10. For 1955 & 1963 interviews see bibl. no.49 and no.31.

11. _____ . An oral history interview. Berkeley, University of California. Regional Oral History Office of the Library, 1960-.
    Interview still in progress at the time of Lange's death. - Approx. 200 p. transcript.

12. _____ & PIRKLE JONES. Death of a valley. *Aperture* v.8, no.3:127-165, 1960.
    Photographs made in 1956-7.

13. _____ . The assignment I'll never forget: migrant mother. *Popular photography* v.46, no.2:42-43, 128, February 1960.

14. _____ . The American farm woman. *Harvester world* v.51, no.11:2-9 ill., November 1960.
    Text & photographs by Lange.

15. _____ [Russell portrait, cover photo of hand photo & tribute] *In* Paper talk: illustrated letters of Charles M. Russell. Ed. by Frederic Renner. Fort Worth, Amon Carter Museum of Western Art, 1962. p.3
    Tribute written by Lange c.1924.

16. _____ . Women of the American farm. *In America illustrated* (U.S.I.A.), Russian ed., no.70:56-61, November 1962.
    Also in Polish ed., no.47:2-7, December 1962. - In Arabic edition, *Al-Hayat,* no.16:18-23, Apr. 1962, as "They are the roots of our country." - All photographs from "The American Country Woman" series.

17. _____. Remembrance of Asia. *In Photography annual 1964.* New York, Ziff-Davis, 1963. p.50-59.
> Text on photographs on p.191,193. - Compiled by editors of *Popular photography.*

18. _____. The American country woman. Fort Worth, Amon Carter Museum of Western Art, 1966. (In preparation).
> Reproduction of Lange's original portfolio including captions. - Intro. by Beaumont Newhall.

SOCIAL DOCUMENTATION BY OTHERS WITH LANGE PHOTOGRAPHS:
(arr. alphabetically):

19. ANDERSON, SHERWOOD. Home town. Photographs by Farm Security photographers. New York, Alliance, 1940. [148]p.
> From "The Face of America" series, ed. by Edwin Rosskam. - 9 photographs by Lange.

20. ISSLER, ANNE ROLLER. Good neighbors lend a hand. Our Mexican workers. *Survey graphic* v.32, no.10:389-394, December 1943.
> Cover photograph. - Includes "Close-up" by Dorothea Lange, p.392, 393.

21. MACLEISH, ARCHIBALD. Land of the free. New York, Harcourt, Brace, 1938. 93 p.
> Reproduces 33 photographs Lange made for the Resettlement Administration.

22. NIXON, HERMAN CLARENCE. Forty acres and steel mules. Chapel Hill, University of North Carolina, 1938. 98 p.
> Includes several Lange photographs.

23. TAYLOR, PAUL SCHUSTER. Again the covered wagon. *Survey graphic* v.24, no.7:348-351, 368, July 1935.
> Photographs by Lange, courtesy of Division of Rural Rehabilitation, California E.R.A.

24. _____. From the ground up. *Survey graphic* v.25, no.9:524-529, 537, 538, September 1936.
> Photographs by Lange for the Resettlement Administration.

25. _____. Our stakes in the Japanese exodus. *Survey graphic* v.31, no.9:372-378, 396, 397, September 1942.
> Photographs, inc.cover, by Lange & Frances Steward for War Relocation Authority.

26. _____ & NORMAN LEON GOLD. San Francisco and the general strike. *Survey graphic* v.23, no.9:404-411, September 1934.
> Frontispiece, p.404, by Lange.

27. U.S. WORKS PROGRESS ADMINISTRATION, DIVISION OF RESEARCH. Rural migration in the United States. 1937.
> Includes Lange photographs.

28. WRIGHT, RICHARD & EDWIN ROSSKAM. 12 million black voices. A folk history of the negro in the United States. New York, Viking, 1941. 152 p.
> Includes 7 photographs by Lange.

ARTICLES ON LANGE (arr. alphabetically):

29. DIXON, DANIEL. Dorothea Lange. *Modern photography* v.16, no.12:68-77, 138-141, December 1952.

30. GRUBER, L. FRITZ. Dorothea Lange. *In* Grosse Photographen unseres jahrhunderts. Darmstadt, Deutsche Buch-Gemeinschaft, 1964. p.68-73 ill.

31. HERZ, NAT. Dorothea Lange in perspective. A reappraisal of the F.S.A. and an interview. *Infinity* v.12, no.4:5-11, April 1963.

32. LORENTZ, PARE. Dorothea Lange: camera with a purpose. *In U.S. camera 1941*

("America") v.1. New York, Duell, Sloan & Pearce, 1940. p.93-116, 229.

Photographs by Lange.

33. MEMORIAL SERVICE FOR DOROTHEA LANGE. Berkeley, [held in] Chapel of the Pacific School of Religion, October 30, 1965. Unpublished transcript of the Memorial service, includes tributes by Allan Temko, Daniel Rhodes Dixon & Christina B. Gardner.

33a. MILLER, WAYNE. Dorothea Lange. [unpublished eulogy]. Distributed by Magnum. October 1965. 2p.

34. MORGAN, WILLARD D., ed. [Lange biography] *In* The encyclopedia of photography. New York, Greystone, 1963. v.11:1950-1952 ill.

35. NEWHALL, BEAUMONT AND NANCY. Dorothea Lange. *In* their Masters of photography. New York, Braziller, 1958. p.140-149.

36. [OBITUARY]. *Berkeley daily gazette,* October 13, 1965.

Also in *Monterey peninsula herald,* October 13, 1965, and *San Francisco chronicle* of same date. - Also *New York times,* October 14 and *San Francisco examiner* October 12, *Nichi Bei times* (San Francisco) October 14, and *Time* October 22.

37. RACANICCHI, PIERO. Dorothea Lange. *Ferrania* v.13, no.5; no pagination, May 1959. 4 pages.

38. _____ Dorothea Lange. *Popular photography, edizione Italiana,* April 1961. p.33-48.

39. SMITH, HENRY HOLMES. Image, obscurity & interpretation. *Aperture* v.5, no.4:136-147, 1957.

On Lange's "Three Women Walking."

40. VAN DYKE, WILLARD. The photographs of Dorothea Lange, a critical analysis. *Camera craft* v.41, no.10:461-467, October 1934.

GENERAL REFERENCE (arr. alphabetically):

41. BUSCH, ARTHUR J. Fellowships for photographers. *Popular photography* v.11, no.4:22-23, 82-83, October 1942.

Subtitled: "Grants from the Guggenheim Foundation enable photographers of outstanding ability to devote a full year to creative work."

42. DOHERTY, ROBERT J., JR. U.S.A.F.S.A. Farm Security Administration photographs of the depression era. *Camera* v.41, no.10:9-51, cover, p.7, October 1962.

43. DURNIAK, JOHN. Focus on Stryker. *Popular photography* v.51, no.3:60-62, 64-65, 80-83, September 1962.

Postscripts on Stryker by Lange and others, p.62-63, 94, ill.

44. ELLIOTT, GEORGE P. Photographs and photographers. *In* his A piece of lettuce. New York, Random House, 1964. p.90-103.

A revised version of his essay in *Commentary,* Dec. 1962, with comments on Lange as a documentary photographer.

45. *FOTOGRAFIE.* F.S.A. Historische Bilddokumente aus den U.S.A. *In* v.19, no.7:246-251, July 1965.

Includes 2 photographs by Lange.

46. GERNSHEIM, HELMUT. Creative photography. Aesthetic trends, 1839-1960. London, Faber & Faber, 1962.

References to Lange, p.214, 221, 240.

47. _____ & ALISON. A concise history of photography. New York, Grosset & Dunlap, 1965.

References to Lange, p.254, 256.

48. HOWE, HARTLEY E. You have seen their pictures. *Survey graphic* v.29, no.4:236-238, April 1940.
   The story of the photographic section of the Farm Security Administration. - Includes 4 photographs by Dorothea Lange.

49. LENZ, HERM. Interview with three greats. *U.S. camera* v.18, no.8:84-87, August 1955.
   Interview with Dorothea Lange, Ansel Adams & Imogen Cunningham.

50. LOUISVILLE. UNIVERSITY OF LOUISVILLE. ALLAN R. HITE ART INSTITUTE. U.S.A.F.S.A. Farm Security Administration photographs of the depression era. Louisville, [The University], 1962. [7]p.
   Jan.15-Feb.24, 1962 - Issued as *Bulletin* v.14, no.3.

51. NEW YORK. MUSEUM OF MODERN ART. The bitter years 1935-1941. Rural America as seen by the photographers of the Farm Security Administration. Ed. by Edward Steichen. New York, [The Museum], 1962. 36 p.
   Oct.18-Nov.25, 1962. - Includes 9 Lange photographs.

52. NEW YORK. MUSEUM OF MODERN ART. The family of man. Created by Edward Steichen. New York, Maco Magazine Corp., 1955. 192 p.
   Jan.24-May 8, 1955. - Includes 9 photographs by Lange.

53. NEWHALL, BEAUMONT. The history of photography from 1839 to the present day. New York, Museum of Modern Art, 1949.
   References to Lange on p.177,178,180,183. - In revised, enlarged second edition (1964) references to her on p.143,146,148,150.

54. POLLACK, PETER. The picture history of photography. New York, Abrams, 1958.
   Reference to Lange on p.351, photograph on p.352.

55. RACANICCHI, PIERO. Farm Security Administration. *In Popular photography, edizione Italiana,* no.2, 1963. No pagination.
   Special issue entitled: Critica e storia della fotografia. - Articles are reprints of some 1962/63 *Popular photography, edizione Italiana* issues. - In part this article reviews Hite Art Institute exhibition of bibl. no.50.

56. ROCHESTER. GEORGE EASTMAN HOUSE. Photography 64. An invitational exhibition co-sponsored by the New York State Exposition & the George Eastman House. Rochester, Eastman House, 1964.
   Circulating exhibition. - Lange photograph on p.23, biography on p.42.

57. SEVERIN, WERNER JOSEPH. Cameras with a purpose: the photojournalists of F.S.A. *Journalism quarterly* v.41, no.2:191-200 ill., spring 1964.

58. _____ Photographic documentation by the Farm Security Administration, 1935-1942. [Unpublished thesis presented to faculty of School of Journalism]. Columbia, University of Missouri, 1959.
   References to Lange on p.10-11, 41, 47.

59. STEICHEN, EDWARD. The F.S.A. photographers. *In U.S. camera 1939.* New York, Morrow & Co., 1938. p.43-65 ill.
   11 photographs by Lange reproduced.

60. _____ Photography. *In* Masters of modern art. Ed. by Alfred H. Barr, Jr. New York, Museum of Modern Art, 1954. p.183-198.

Reproduces "A Depression Breadline, San Francisco. 1933" by Lange. p.195.

61. U.S. PRESIDENT'S COMMITTEE. Report of the President's Committee. Farm tenancy. February 1937. (Supt. of Public Documents edition J129512)
Includes photographs by Lange.